WE

NEED

to

TALK

Communicating Through
Difficult Situations
in Four Easy Steps

Suzanne Seifert Groves

Black Rose Writing | Texas

The author grants the final approval for this literary material.

First printing

This is a work of fiction. Names, characters, businesses, places, events,
and incidents are either the products of the author's imagination or
used in a fictitious manner. Any resemblance to actual persons, living or
dead, or actual events is purely coincidental.

ISBN: 978-1-68513-295-8
PUBLISHED BY BLACK ROSE WRITING
www.blackrosewriting.com

Printed in the United States of America
Suggested Retail Price (SRP) $15.95

We Need to Talk is printed in Cambria

*As a planet-friendly publisher, Black Rose Writing does its best to eliminate
unnecessary waste to reduce paper usage and energy costs, while never
compromising the reading experience. As a result, the final word count vs. page
count may not meet common expectations.

This book is lovingly dedicated to my late mother, the Honorable Judge Charlene M. Seifert, who taught me at an early age the power of using my words to express myself (whether she agreed with me or not), and to my daughter, Gabrielle Cottraux, whose talent for communication will forever serve her well.

"The single biggest problem in communication is the illusion that it has taken place."
–George Bernard Shaw

"The two words 'information' and 'communication' are often used interchangeably, but they signify quite different things. Information is giving out; communication is getting through."
–Sydney J. Harris

"It sounds so trite but in relationships, you have to communicate."
–Peter Krause

"The art of communication is the language of leadership."
–James Humes

WE
NEED
To
TALK

Introduction

In my thirty-five year career as a communications strategist and executive coach, I've seen firsthand that just like many people believe they have a sparkling wit or can bust impressive moves on the dance floor, most leaders think their communications skills, if not rock solid, are good enough. The general truth is, these leaders have ascended in their careers despite their communications skills, not because of them.

Let's start with the title of this book: *We Need to Talk.* Provocative, right? Here's why. Few people wish to speak these words, and no one ever wants to hear them; they're the equivalent of a *Danger Ahead* sign posted just before a sharp curve which, if poorly navigated, will propel your car (or your career) right off the cliff. Never begin a conversation, difficult or otherwise, with these four words unless your intent is to incapacitate your recipient from understanding what you need to communicate.

The purpose of this book is to help you, no matter your background, your position, or your relationships, to communicate through any challenge, such that your audience can metabolize your message in a mutually beneficial way. By the time you finish this book and begin applying the four-step methodology I've explained, I promise you'll feel relieved to have such a simple tool at your disposal.

1. It's Not About You

From the moment we took our first raspy breaths as adorable little humans, we were imbued with innate mechanisms that enabled us to communicate our needs. Hungry? *Howl!* Loaded diaper? *Cry!* Sleepy but unable to nod off? *Sob!* Teething? *Cry, drool, and chew on our knuckles.* Frightened? *Scream!* Frustrated? *Scream louder, while possibly stomping, throwing things, or hurling ourselves to the floor.* Hurt? *Hold breath for five seconds before shrieking.* You get the idea. We were exclamation points trapped in chubby little bodies. Our primal communications skills signaled our need for attention – our guttural complaints were requests in disguise.

Depending on your parentage, your number in the birth order, your environment, your cultural mores, your genes, and a host of other factors, somewhere in the early toddler years, you acquired words to express your questions, needs, and desires. Your emergent communication style may have been guided by parents and teachers who encouraged you to 'use your words.' Or it may have been impacted by an outmoded but still existent belief that children are to be seen and not heard.

If the adults around you were conflict-avoidant or emotionally unstable, you may have learned to tiptoe around saying what you needed to say for the greater peace. In all likelihood though, you probably didn't spend time thinking about – or learning – how best to communicate so that you connected evenly and positively with a fellow human.

There are thousands of books about interpersonal communication, covering topics like body language, facial expressions, phrases to avoid, colloquialisms that can be mis-construed, overcoming language barriers, and more. Few, if any, get down to brass tacks about communicating in a manner that aligns with brain chemistry and neurotransmission while providing a clear playbook. Because here's the deal: effective communication simply isn't hard if you start with one fundamental premise: It's all about you, but it's not about you.

Wait, what?

That's right. Effective communication is all about you as the communicator, but it's not about you as the recipient. If your intent is to make a request, course-correct, discipline, advise, or provide new direction, you won't achieve your desired outcome if your audience is so freaked out they can't hear you.

Despite our fervent wishes that people pay less attention to what we say and more to our fundamental intent, it doesn't work that way. No one can see into our brain to know our meaning. Nor can we count on T-mail – the information we send telepathically to the receiver with hopes they will automagically catch our drift. We want our messages served up in such a way that we don't have to step into the blurry courage-zone to deliver them ourselves.

Straight talk: daily life requires us to connect with others. Be they our parents, our children, our bosses, our employees, our spouses, our friends, snarky Customer Service reps, our doctors, our hairstylists, our mechanics, the IRS – we can't avoid the need for messy conversations.

We can't avoid having to share information people may not want to hear.

We can't seek shelter from having to reset certain relationships.

We can't slink into the closet with our blankie when we need to have a difficult talk.

We can't let ourselves down by communicating ineffectively – not if we hope to have a sane and stable life with sane and stable relationships.

Years ago, I stumbled across an affirmation that I've offered up to my daughter, my friends, my colleagues, and even myself when I choose to listen: *Own your space.* I've interpreted that to mean: stand firmly in what you believe, don't be afraid to communicate the hard stuff, don't let yourself down by suppressing or avoiding what needs to be expressed, and trust your intentions are for the good, not the destructive.

Your ability to have the tough chat in a way that leads to a positive experience for yourself and your recipient starts with you. And it resides in your intent.

2. What Did You Mean by That?

Though we are highly evolved beings with extraordinary brains and limitless capacity to process information, we get triggered fairly easily. It's because we listen for and often assume hidden intent.

We also understand the concept of passive-aggression – running rampant like a half-naked toddler through Walmart anymore – and often infuse into what we think we hear. Sometimes, we also may add a dollop of passive-aggression – the Snark Shark – to what we *say* because it comes more naturally than processing all the emotion conjoined with the intent of what needs to be communicated.

This biased filter amplifies in conjunction with our relationship to the person speaking to us, or with whom we need to have a chat.

I once had an employee who was sufficiently talented, but ridiculously difficult to manage because his first reaction to any type of coaching or critique was immediate defensive-ness, which then spiraled into a Snark Shark frenzy.

Boss Me: "In the future, I'd like you to come to me first if one of our team members becomes hospitalized, so we can manage the communications process together.

Employee Shark: "What did I do wrong?"

Slightly Irked Me: "I did not say you did anything wrong. I'm saying that in the future, I'd like you to come to me first."

Snarky Sharky: "What you're telling me to do isn't in our policy manual and I don't under-stand why you're telling me what to do."

Annoyed Boss Me: "As the head of this division and as your supervisor, I'm simply stating that this is my expectation of how you'll handle something like this differently in the future."

Jaws: "I'm hanging up and we can take this up with HR."

Very Aggravated Me: "That's fine." (It's not fine. It's never fine when people say, "It's fine.")

I had not yet employed the playbook I'm revealing here, and I should have known better, particularly as our relationship had been prickly since I was promoted from peer to boss shortly after joining the organization. Doesn't matter though. The issue at hand was that he had failed to notify me in a timely manner about a sudden and tragic medical condition of one of the members of my division (and his direct report), who subsequently died. Accordingly, nerves were frayed and emotions heightened on both ends of the phone. Yet, while I was fighting through my bias ('he's a difficult person to manage and an even harder person with whom to communicate'), he was reclining into his Lazy-Boy of resentment that I'm his boss at all. Though he didn't ask, "What do you mean by that?" his reaction said otherwise. He thought the conversation was a referendum on his existence.

It didn't have to be that way. Knowing what I know, I could have handled it much better.

Avoid Snark Sharks: Don't Be One, and by all means, Don't Bait One. Snarknado can get ugly, fast.

3. *What Are You Really Saying?*

Since I can remember, I've loved the water. I began swimming at an early age, or rather running like a crazed ostrich, hurling myself in the deep end when my parents weren't watching, then spluttering for air and doggy-paddling to the side. Water was fun and some chances were worth taking.

Swimming in murky waters though can lead to unpleasant encounters. I nearly lost a finger to a barracuda in Cozumel. Margaritas may or may not have been involved. I stayed calm, it grew bored and swam off, and that night my bestie and I ordered grilled barracuda to 'own our space.'

Embarking upon a possibly messy discussion without a clear understanding of your intent and your desired outcomes is like jumping into a Louisiana swamp with a pocket full of hotdogs. You might survive it, appendages intact. Or you might get dragged underwater and devoured like a human burrito.

Intent has two components: understanding *why* you need to say what needs to be said and, assuming your motives are good, taking responsibility for *how* the recipient processes the information in a way that is beneficial for both of you.

At this point, you may recall other books you've read that suggest what other people think of you and how other people react to you is about THEM and to a degree, that's true. However, if the relationship is important to you – because it's related to your job (it's good to live indoors and afford food), your partner, other family members, friends, or anyone else with whom a peaceful understanding is preferable to ill will and acrimony – your intent is not only important, it's mission-critical.

When I first developed and began teaching this communications methodology, I was working for a technology company with offices in sixty countries. For corporate cost efficiency, we offshored more and more of our software development and programming over the years – a great bottom-line move, but one that revealed significant cultural differences in people's perspectives on leadership.

In a nutshell, the Millennials who had grown up in formerly Communist countries were not hard-wired to move up the corporate ladder, yet we needed to groom future leaders so that our ex-pat executives could return to the U.S.

Perhaps the most important role of true leadership is effective communication, so I was asked to take my show on the road to Poland, where I joined a few other corporate specialists (representing several different leadership dimensions) to help coach these high-potential leaders

I'm a creative, a marketer, a communicator, an off-the-charts extrovert with enough ADD to be dangerous, and enough passion for my work to be able to capture at least initial audience interest when I begin a presentation. So I went into the first day of sessions feeling pretty positive, honestly. *I got this!*

My audiences over the course of the next three days consisted of young, predominantly male, Polish software developers who just wanted to get the information they needed so they could go on to the next session. They were lovely people and appreciated my speaking a few, possibly botched words in Polish. Several participants even gently offered pronunciation tips. But it was clear they wanted me to Get. On. With. It.

So, I did. I began my presentation with a discussion of why effective communication is vital for leaders and absolutely essential to a business's success. I shared some interesting facts about the real bottom-line impact of poor communication (they liked the data part). And I assured them, like a D-List celeb hawking the latest gadget on late-night TV, that what I was about to teach them would change the trajectory of their careers if they put it to work.

They looked collectively skeptical, so I shook up the order I originally had planned for the presentation and asked if there were any volunteers for a role-playing activity. I wasn't sure if role-playing was a thing in Poland, but you use what you've got. After a minute or two, during which I offered up a few 'pleases' in Polish, a tall young man stood up and approached me cautiously. I smiled and told him that we were going to run through a scenario in which I was his boss and he was my employee. He nodded confidently, chin raised and smiling as widely as a contestant on the Wheel of Fortune.

"Jani, I need you to pack up your office by three today. There have been some changes."

Jani suddenly didn't look too happy.

"What's happening? Why?" Jani's eyes were wide because even though we were pretending, stuff like this actually happened at our company. Frequently.

"You're being moved to a different group," I responded.

"But why? Did I do something wrong?" His body language conveyed terror.

"It's not so much that, as we need to make a change," I said.

"Why?"

"It just appears your skills may be more useful in the other department," I said, nodding as if to say, "Okay? Get it? Are we done here?"

Jani paused for a minute before asking what office he was moving to. I made something up, and he nodded again. Then, "What are you really saying?"

BOOM. There it is. The innate fear that I, as his leader, had dragged him down into the murky waters of ambiguity where he would surely drown or be consumed as a delectable treat by The Unknown.

I thanked Jani for being a good sport, assured him that to the best of my knowledge, he wasn't getting moved anywhere at all except when it was time for us to go to lunch, and then launched into my discussion about intent.

This line would not have played well in Poland for all the cultural reasons, but I have found it useful in teaching this methodology on this side of the Pond.

Ambiguity: what happens in vagueness, stays in vagueness.

Before delving deeper into intent as your communications anchor, let's talk about hijacking.

4. We've Been Hijacked

I was a child in the sixties and seventies – interesting times for sure – and I remember three key themes that permeated the news on one of the three network TV stations. First, Watergate. Man, that rodeo seemed to go on forever. The second, and one that I found particularly fascinating: UFOs. Many a summer night, my neighborhood gang and I would sit in one of our front yards and peer up to the sky, eagerly awaiting an extraterrestrial visitor. The third, one that I indeed found terrifying, was hijacking. In my child's mind, it seemed Bad Guys were stealing planes and demanding they be flown elsewhere at least once a week. (Interesting fact: Between 1968 and 1972, more than 130 American airplanes were hijacked.)

There is no positive form of hijacking. Hi-jacking always means seizing control that is not freely given.

The **cerebral cortex** is the area of the brain that processes information, while the **cerebrum** controls our emotions and what we see and hear. Like a radar, the **amygdala** constantly monitors the environment for threatening stimuli. If it activates, the cerebral cortex goes on strike. This is known as Amygdala Hijack, and when it happens, we revert to our most primal selves. We fight, freeze, flee or fawn. None of these leads to a favorable outcome when we're simply navigating a conversation.

Fight. The hijacked brain that's poised to fight knows no bounds, and the collateral damage can be staggering and often irreparable. Imagine a cornered wild animal. It turns into a battle and can get very messy.

Freeze. When the hijacked brain freezes, the senses shut down. A cold dread snakes down the spine, breathing all but stops, palms sweat, and there's an inability to consider the next move. It can take time for the frozen person to thaw, after which they're either going to have to revisit the conversation or give it up altogether.

Flee: This person will run away from the perceived threat or run toward a perceived solution.

This employee might quit on the spot, file a complaint against you with HR, or gobble up all their sick time because they're avoiding the situation.

I once had a horse that was extremely gentle except when spooked, which happened periodically despite my careful handling. Once, while walking him through a new jumping course so he would become acclimated, the wind caught hold of a tarp covering a hay bale. He startled, then broke into a full gallop as I desperately tried to avoid crashing into a jump we couldn't handle. He ended up tossing me, and I broke my elbow. Flee mode can be dangerous even when you're not the one running.

Fawn. This person gives in and sacrifices their own well-being for another's, particularly to avoid conflict. In trying to be a people pleaser, one who fawns is trading their authentic reaction for expected protection and favor.

Understanding how the parts of the brain work together to process information while simultaneously assessing possible threat is fundamental to effective communication.

5. I Told You

You're presumably reading this book because you're a good person who wants to communicate effectively and promote harmony and understanding. If, instead, you're someone who wishes to maintain the upper hand in your relationships by instilling fear through your intimidating communications style, stop reading and go sharpen your fangs.

When we need to communicate about challenging subjects, it's important to consider our intent *before* we open our mouth or put fingers to the keyboard. Steven Covey famously advised in *The Seven Habits of Highly Effective People* to 'begin with the end in mind.' What do you want to accomplish?

Rollo Reece May, an American psychologist and author, wrote 'Communication leads to community…

to understanding, intimacy, and mutual valuing.' Our most powerful gift is verbal communication – our key to real human connection.

Yet, it isn't that simple. George Bernard Shaw wrote, 'The single biggest problem in communication is the illusion that it has taken place.' Just because you got things off your chest doesn't mean you communicated effectively in a manner that aligned with your *cognitive* (versus *emotional*) intent.

Again, what do you want and/or need to accomplish? Do you want your receiver to process new information, to consider a different perspective, to have greater confidence in you as a leader, partner, or parent; to feel more optimistic, to change the way they work, or to simply be informed?

In the context of our work relationships, intentional communication is critical in guiding another's behavior toward better understanding, engagement, and receptivity. Why is this important? Engaged employees will give you discretionary work effort, going the extra mile, because they have internalized the values of the organization, they understand how their work contributes to the big picture, and they trust their leaders. Organizations with highly engaged employees regularly see greater productivity and post greater profits than those whose employees are disengaged or checked out. If you think about an organization as a living being – a complex ecosystem – you can understand the same Amygdala Hijack that can seize an individual also can seize a group. When this happens, nothing good comes from it.

Within this context, engagement is a three-step process that begins with awareness – the individual's knowledge about the subject at hand. Take the challenging topic of cost-cutting measures. The CEO (or CFO or COO) who understands that reducing operating expenses is a team sport will go beyond announcing the tactic – "we need to reduce costs by 20% in the next six months" – and help employees process the information in a non-threatening manner. Too many leaders think that communication starts and ends with, "I told you."

Savvy leaders want engaged employees to next internalize the message – in this instance, 'Okay, we need to cut costs. Got it. I can be part of the solution. Here's what I can do in my role to help. Ready, Captain!'

When the employee is thoroughly engaged because they feel part of a team working toward a solution, it gets better. "Here we go, finding ways to cut costs in order to help our company survive and ultimately flourish. Hey, I've worked up some ideas – can I share them with you?" TOUCHDOWN. HOMERUN. GOAL!

We want people in our personal lives to be engaged with us as well. For example, you may find yourself needing to say, "Honey, we need to be more careful with money right now." You've made your partner *aware* that *you* think you both need to watch your coins. But what if they've assumed passive-aggressive intent and think you're accusing them of driving you toward bankruptcy with their shoe obsession? Or they feel resentful because they work too and would like some say in the matter? Or they feel alarmed because they've had an Amygdala Hijack and think there's something scarier you're not telling them?

You didn't help them internalize the information in a way they could engage with you and work towards a solution.

How could you have engaged them as an employee, or in solidarity as your spouse, when it came to these challenges? By carefully identifying the outcomes you wanted or needed from your intentional communications approach.

6. I Know, I Know

At the heart of a good relationship is active trust. Not the concept of trust, i.e., I'm supposed to trust you because you're my boss, spouse, parent, neighbor, doctor – but a trust based on best intentions. You want the best for that person.

As a leader, spouse, parent and beyond, you will need to communicate a difficult message at some point, and you will only achieve your desired outcome/s if your audience trusts you. And we trust people we believe have a full grasp of the situation.

Thus, the first component of your message should be grounded in knowledge, because that will help your audience feel safe, or at least not threatened. This means using phrases like:

"I know..."

"I understand..."

"I'm sure…"

"I'm aware that…"

"I've been told that…"

Beginning with what you know sets the desired tone that your perspective can be trusted, ensuring your audience will listen, process, internalize, and engage.

Using the example of corporate cost-cutting measures to keep the entity afloat, here's how it should begin:

"I know there are rumors afloat that our company may be in trouble due to a significant decrease in annual sales, and that these rumors have created some concerns about what this means for the future of our company. And I know many of you may be thinking it's time to start looking for other employment." *Read: I'm a leader with my finger on the pulse of this organization and I get that folks are worried. But please lean forward because I'm going to tell you what's really happening.*

Or you believe your family needs to limit spending for a while as your job may be uncertain.

"Honey, I know we share a love of traveling, dining out, and occasionally splurging on a new piece of art. I also know we share a vision for what our retirement looks like once the kids are grown, and that together we'll do what's needed to make that happen." *Read: I know we're united in this crazy thing called marriage and now we really have to pull together and I'm confident we'll do so.*

Or, you're a parent and you need to tell your child that you're seriously ill.

"Sweetheart, I know you've been worried about how tired I've been lately, and I've seen you take on a lot more responsibilities around the house without being asked. I'm sure this has been bothering you more than you've said." *Read: I see you and even though I don't feel well, you're still my priority.*

Or, you might need to not be wakened at 8 a.m. on a Saturday by your neighbor's compulsive leaf-blowing.

"Hey, neighbor! I know you take incredible pride in your yard and garden – always so lovely! I also know that every Saturday, you like to get cracking early, before it gets too warm outside. Totally understand." *Read: I know you're a conscientious person or you wouldn't be so disciplined with this weekly practice. Here I am, your non-threatening neighbor, seeing you and your great work ethic.*

Beginning with what you know is the beginning of your intentional communication to follow. Regardless of what you need to communicate, by using knowledge as the foundation – what you know, what your audience knows – you are activating your receiver's frontal lobe – the part that processes information – instead of poking their amygdala to react.

7. Here's The Deal

You've established your understanding of the situation at hand and created a calm space in which to have the necessary conversation by beginning with what you know, which may include what your audience may have heard or be concerned about, and that their point of view may differ from what you're about to express.

The next step in your intentional, effective communication is to transition to the 'Real Deal' – information that clarifies the situation and helps guide your audience to think differently.

You may think that sounds manipulative. It's not. This is about helping your audience to process information in a non-threatening manner so your employee can manage through ambiguity, or your spouse can calmly work with you to sort out family challenges, or your child feels they're being treated with respect even as you're navigating a health scare, or that your neighbor doesn't start leaf-blowing even earlier each Saturday to tick you off.

Returning to our corporate example that began with what you know, here's how to move to the information-sharing section:

"I know there are rumors afloat that our company may be in trouble due to a significant decrease in annual sales, and that these rumors have created some concerns about what this means for our company and our future. And I know many of you may be thinking it's time to start looking for other employment.

"Here's what I can share with you. It's true that we've seen a 25 percent decrease in sales, in part because of supply chain challenges and in part because of new product entries in the market. Because of the combination of slower fulfillment by our global partners and growing competition in our space, we have identified measures we can take to shore up our bottom line and thus, ensure our operational continuity. Those measures do include cost-cutting by up to 25%, but we do not anticipate any near-term reductions in staff if we can reduce other non-essential expenditures in the next six months."

In the space of four sentences, you have affirmed that while the company is not in trouble, there are changes needed to protect the bottom line. You provided important context – supply chain challenges that contribute to product availability and increased competition in your industry – to bring your employees up to speed with why cost-cutting measures are necessary. You have trusted them enough to share the real deal. Finally, in this critical level-setting component of your message, you have addressed the true elephant in the room – "Should I clean out my desk before or after I get my pink slip?" – by stating that in the near term, personnel changes are not in the mix.

At this point, your employees may be nervous. But they're not jumping ship because you've conveyed genuine leadership through your thoughtful and non-threatening approach to the message.

Moving to our spousal example where perhaps you've received a message about cost-cutting measures at work and wish to take personal financial precautions, here's how you would transition from what you know, to what you need your spouse to know:

"Honey, I know we share a love of traveling, dining out, and occasionally splurging on a new piece of art. I also know we share a vision for what our retirement looks like once the kids are grown, and that together we'll do what's needed to make that happen."

"Here's the thing. Our CEO has told us that, due to decreased sales revenues, we're going to have to cut corporate costs pretty significantly over the next six months. He told us that, for now, he doesn't envision the need to let people go, so that's a good thing. That said, we're carrying some debt that would prove challenging if I lose my job in the next year. The best thing for our future is that we're a bit more frugal with our spending and save as much as possible, just in case. That doesn't mean we're in trouble, it means we're being smart."

By communicating with your partner about what needs to change, you're giving them not only your trust, but your respect in navigating the unexpected together. As is commonly known, if not always acknowledged, financial concerns are one of the most challenging issues couples navigate. Communicating effectively and with the intention of fostering a *we're in this together* mindset will go a long way to strengthening your relationship while addressing the most pressing concern.

When it comes to our children, most of us are hard-wired to shield them from life's unpleasantries, particularly when it comes to our own vulnerabilities. We want them to see us as strong and capable so they feel safe. They need us to be strong and capable so they can focus on being kids. Yet, there are circumstances when, in shielding them from what's really happening, we rob them of valuable lessons about how to manage crises with grace and dignity, and how to pull together when the going gets tough.

Looking at a situation in which you've just received a medical diagnosis that will result in ongoing treatment, possible hospitalization or surgery, and a change in your ability to participate in activities for the foreseeable future, putting things into perspective is critical:

"Sweetheart, I know you've been worried about how tired I've been lately, and I've seen you take on a lot more responsibilities around the house without being asked. I'm sure this has been bothering you more than you've said."

"First, thank you for helping out. I'm proud of you. After telling Dr Jones how I felt, she ran some tests. I'm probably going to need surgery because I have a lump in my thyroid gland (*gesturing where the thyroid gland is*) that concerns her a bit. Right now, we don't know if it's something that may require further treatment, but we're getting it taken care of to be safe. So, next week, I'll be going to the hospital for a minor procedure to find out what's going on."

Any child hearing that a parent might be ill is sure to experience some alarm, whether they express it or not. By calmly inviting your child into your reality, you are conveying your respect for this person as a vital member of the family so they feel safe asking questions, versus having to put on a stoic veneer. And, you're signaling that you believe they're smart enough and strong enough to handle adult situations without bearing the burden of having to fix anything, because you've got this.

Finally, our early morning leaf-blower. We want to have positive relationships with those proximal to us, especially at home, even though we may not be buddies. Here's how you might put your need for a later leaf-blowing start time into context:

"Hey, neighbor! I know you take incredible pride in your yard and garden – always so lovely! I also know that every Saturday, you like to get cracking early, before it gets too warm outside. Totally understand. This heat is crazy!

"I'm not sure you know, but I work until about 9pm every night during the week at the hospital, and I'm up early on Sunday to get to church, so Saturday is the only day I can really sleep in. Between work and kids, I need that extra rest to stay healthy and manage all my responsibilities! When you're tending to your yard with the leaf-blower at 8am, it wakes up the household – children, husband, dogs and as a result, me – and I can't get the rest I need. I'd like to ask, quite respectfully, if you would consider either a later time or a different day to tend to your magnificent garden?"

The truth is, your neighbor could angrily retort that he, too, has responsibilities and that this is the time that works best for him. But that would be a pretty crappy thing to do and by approaching him as a kind human being who only wants one day a week to charge your batteries, you're inviting him to be a kind human.

You might think your intentional communications, are finished at this point. *Au contraire*! You've carefully positioned yourself as someone who understands the concerns, issues, and situation at hand, and you've offered a message based on accurate information. The most important steps are still to come.

8. I Feel You

Despite the fact that you've carefully organized your message (with your primary intention of preventing Amygdala Hijack) by starting with what you know, have heard or have observed, followed by a clear presentation of the facts, your audience still has some emotions about the situation. To ignore this vital piece of the equation denies their human-ness.

In the work world, we often overlook the three-dimensionality of our colleagues and team members, because we've been socialized to show up as good corporate soldiers and do what is asked without emotional response. "I'm here to do a job, not win a popularity contest." This lack of workplace emotional intelligence is typical of an older generation. Today, positive workplace relationships are often more important than individual task performance. Though this rigid leadership dynamic has eased over the years, thanks largely to Millennials and their unwavering skepticism of authority, we still see vestiges of 'command and control' and 'because I said so' in the corporate space.

Companies that invest in supporting their employees' emotional well-being outperform those that don't for the simple reason that people want to be valued in tangible ways and will go above and beyond when they're appreciated. This doesn't mean ping-pong tables in every break room or pet therapy every other Friday, though these are certainly nice touches. It means recognizing the whole-ness of your team, emotions and all.

Using our ongoing examples to understand how you would weave in an acknowledgement of emotion, let's start with the corporate cost-cutting conversation:

"I know there are rumors afloat that our company may be in trouble due to a significant decrease in annual sales, and that these rumors have created some concerns about what this means for our company and our future. And I know many of you may be thinking it's time to start looking for other employment.

"Here's what I can share with you. It's true that we've seen a 25 percent decrease in sales, in part because of supply chain challenges and in part because of continued new product entries. The combination of slower fulfillment by our global partners and growing competition in our space has led us to identify measures we can take to shore up our bottom line and thus ensure our operational continuity. Those measures include cost-cutting measures by up to 25% but we do not anticipate any near-term reductions in staff if we can reduce other non-essential expenditures in the next six months."

"Clearly, this is *hard to hear.* For so many of you who have given tirelessly of yourselves to build this company, you're likely *feeling some apprehension* about what seems like an uncertain future for us. While I, too, am *concerned* about our current situation, I am *not worried* because I have great trust in this extraordinary team and your collective commitment to keeping this company strong. I feel *reassured* knowing you will use your innovative thinking and teamwork to help us meet our cost-cutting goals in a way that is right for the company and in a way that does not cause us to sacrifice our fundamental value propositions."

In this third and most important component of your message, you've effectively outed your-self as a genuine human being while honoring the humanness of your audience in a manner that equalizes the team. You've offered your own vulnerability, immediately balanced by your confidence as a leader. You've also given your team permission to have an emotional response to the changes necessary for your company's solvency. Finally, you've signaled an invitation to everyone in the audience that they, regardless of title or position, can be part of the solution. You just gave them inspiration, which lights up the problem-solving (frontal lobe) area of the brain. Bravo!

In our personal lives, assuming our relationships are relatively healthy, it's a bit easier to address the emotional side of difficult situations because we've achieved some *intimacy equity* over time. And if you haven't, it's never too late.

You've now told your spouse that due to cost-cutting measures at work, it may be time to follow suit at home. Here's how your message might continue:

"Honey, I know you and I share a love of traveling, dining out and occasionally splurging on a new piece of art. I also know we share a vision for what our retirement looks like, once the kids are grown, and that together we'll do what's needed to make that happen.

"The thing is, our CEO just told us that due to decreased sales revenues, we're going to have to cut corporate costs over the next six months. He told us that for now, he doesn't envision the need to let people go, so that's a good thing. That said, we're carrying some debt that would prove challenging if for some reason I lose my job in the next year. The best thing for our future is that we are a bit more frugal with our spending and save as much as possible, just in case. That doesn't mean we're in trouble; it means we're being smart.

"I *wish* we weren't in this position right now and I understand this may *feel unsettling.* It does to me, too. I have *confidence* in our ability to weather any storm together, although this isn't one yet. I *hope* that being more mindful about how we manage our money strengthens us and gives us opportunities to be more creative and resourceful – this actually might be fun! I want to *reassure* you though, that we'll manage through together, like we always do."

By expressing your authentic emotions – both concern and confidence – in a non-threatening manner, you've created a safe space for your spouse to respond and react as well. Shifting the narrative of imposed change (no more vacations for a while) to one of positive collaboration enables your partner to be part of the solution. They may decide to sacrifice their online shoe habit or take on a side gig or pack Ramen for lunch for the next six months – that's not the point (not yet, anyway). As with the earlier corporate example, your partner's brain is now processing what positive change might look like instead of how frightening the future might appear.

Speaking of the frontal lobe, it's commonly known that with children, that critical part of the brain is not fully developed until the early to mid-twenties. When having a serious conversation about a potentially alarming subject with a younger person or child, the time you spend addressing the emotions entwined with the situation must be your area of greatest focus and care.

You've now told your child that you will be having a surgical procedure to get to the bottom of why you've been so fatigued lately. As the parent, you clearly don't want to stoke your child's fears, yet you want to be honest because you're modeling – in this and so many other moments – the best way to handle difficult times. Here's how your conversation can continue:

"Sweetheart, I know you've been worried about how tired I've been lately, and I've seen you take on a lot more responsibilities around the house without being asked. I'm sure this has been bothering you more than you've said.

"Thank you for helping out. I'm proud of you. After telling Dr Jones how I was feeling, she decided to run some tests. I'm going to need minor surgery because I have a lump in my thyroid gland (*gesturing where the thyroid gland is*) that concerns her a bit. Right now, we don't know if it's something that may require further treatment, but we're getting it taken care of to be safe. So, next week, I'll be going to the hospital to have a minor procedure so we can find out what's going on.

"This feels kinda *scary*, doesn't it? It does to me, too. It's okay to be *afraid*, but I promise you that this family is strong enough to handle anything, right? I'm also *excited* that this will help me feel better, which will give me more energy to do all the things we *love* to do together."

Depending on your child's age, they may be sobbing or they may be glowering. Yet, they're also seeing you as a three-dimensional human being who gets scared and still maintains confidence in the solid family structure. You've expressed the upside of your surgery – feeling better – and painted a picture of better times ahead. You've created a space for them to safely react while staying close to you.

Hopefully, your discussion with Mr. Early Bird Leaf Blower won't feel quite as emotional – for you, anyway – yet you still need to recognize that he's going to feel something about your request. Give this a look:

"Hey, neighbor! I know you take incredible pride in your yard and garden – always so lovely! I also know that every Saturday, you like to get cracking early, before it gets too warm outside. Totally understand. This heat is crazy!

"I'm not sure you know, but I work until about 9pm every night during the week at the hospital, and I'm up early on Sunday to get to church, so Saturday is the only day I can really sleep in. Between work and raising my kids, I need that extra rest to stay healthy and manage my responsibilities at home and at work! When you're tending your yard with the leaf-blower at 8am, it wakes up the household – children, husband, dogs and as a result, me – and I can't get back to sleep. I'd like to ask, quite respectfully, if you would consider either a later time or a different day to tend to your magnificent garden?

"I was *worried* about having this conversation because the last thing I would want to do is to *offend* you or *upset* you; you are such nice neighbors. And, I don't want to be one of those people, you know? I really *appreciate* your being open to changing your schedule just a little bit, and for being so *kind* in this discussion. And I sure would *love* your secret for getting your hydrangeas to survive this heat!"

Look at you, all pulled together and having a touchy chat with your neighbor! In the world of social media, including sites specific for neighborhoods, it would have been so much easier to post a nasty-gram about your un-named neighbor who's driving you bat-shit crazy with his obvious OCD every Saturday morning. You might even have attributed some additional nasty characteristic – "if you knew his wife, you'd know why he doesn't want to lounge around on a Saturday morning" – to underscore your righteousness in the face of his obvious terribleness.

But you didn't. Instead, you owned your space and shared your apprehension about speaking to him directly, coupled with your expectation that he would be kind and your appreciation for him as a neighbor. At this point, he could tell you off, but most likely, he won't. Instead, he will see you for who you are: a mature adult capable of setting boundaries to protect yourself. He'll also be considering – via his frontal lobe – whether to share his special recipe for hydrangea fertilizer.

You've now learned how to frame important conversations beginning with a statement of knowledge or understanding, followed by a presentation of facts, information or truths that establish the narrative, balanced by a very human recognition of the authentic emotions – yours and theirs – naturally intrinsic to the situation. You're almost there. One key component remains, and this is where the magic truly happens.

9. Do What?

Joel Barker is a business guru who introduced the concept of paradigm shifts in the 1980s as the catalyst for positive organizational transformation. He has spoken to millions of people around the world and his films have been watched by hundreds of millions more. While I've not directly encountered his work, I know it has infused a good share of my corporate experiences and so many of his words ring true, not the least of which is this: *Vision without action is merely a dream. Action without vision just passes the time. Vision with action can change the world.*

Reviewing all four of our communications examples thus far, in every scenario you've established a vision for your audience about the situation at hand (what you know and what you need your audience to know), and you've given your audience permission to have their own emotional responses, just as you have shared your feelings, too. You can't sit there having your Kumbaya moment for long though, otherwise nothing changes. Your audience may consider what you've said and simply continue doing what they've always done, which won't get you to active solutions and tangible change.

Quoting Barker again: *A leader is a person you will follow to a place you wouldn't go by yourself.*

Where are you taking them and what are the steps to get there? You've established their trust; now, you need to inspire their move-ment toward the optimal outcome.

Let's start with the cost-cutting discussion. Here's how you bring it home for the team:

"I know there are rumors afloat that our company may be in trouble due to a significant decrease in annual sales, and that these rumors have created some concerns about what this means for our company and our future. And I know many of you may be thinking it's time to start looking for other employment.

"Here's what I can share with you. It's true that we've seen a 25 percent decrease in sales, in part because of supply chain challenges and in part because of new product entries. The combination of slower fulfillment by our global partners and growing competition in our space, while somewhat beyond our control, has led us to identify measures to shore up our bottom line and ensure our operational continuity. Those measures include cost-cutting by up to 25%, but we do not anticipate any near-term reductions in staff if we can reduce other non-essential expenditures in the next six months.

"Clearly, this is hard to hear and for many of you who have given tirelessly of yourselves to build this company up, you're likely feeling some apprehension about what seems like an uncertain future for us. While I, too, am concerned about our current situation, I am not worried because I trust this extraordinary team and your collective commitment to keeping this company strong. I know you will use your innovative thinking and teamwork to help us meet our cost-cutting goals in a way that is right for the company and does not cause us to sacrifice our fundamental value propositions.

"Here's how I propose we start. First, I'd like each of you who manages a divisional budget to identify what costs you can cut without any impact to our operations – review travel plans that can be tabled, subscriptions that can be canceled, professional memberships that don't add value, and most of all, entertainment expenses. Please provide me your written recommendations for what can be eliminated – for now – from your budget by this Friday. Next, I'd like you to meet with your team members to brainstorm additional cost-saving measures for the company and submit them to me via email by the following Friday. The team that delivers the most effective cost-cutting strategies in a quantifiable way will be rewarded with paid time off, above what you've already accrued!

"I'm going to work with IT to establish a dedicated email box for you to submit questions or observations, and I'll have our Corporate Communications team provide a weekly summary on our company Intranet. I want to keep our lines of communication open and celebrate our successes along the way.

"Finally, if our situation changes in any way, or I receive new information that may have some bearing on our company goals, you will hear from me in real time so we continue to navigate our future together.

"I am honored and humbled to work with an outstanding team and I appreciate your collaboration and cooperation at an important time for this company. Are there any questions?"

Whew. You did it. You shared the vision and you've guided the immediate action needed such that your employees are already thinking about moving to a paperless environment, chucking all the Styrofoam cups, and planning what they're going to do with their paid time off because their team is going to win! The truth is, your entire staff will win because they've internalized your message – that the company needs to make some changes with their collective help – and they're now fully engaged in the solution.

And here's the thing: your message did not come across as a dictate, but rather as an invitation for your team – regardless of position or title – to pull together for the good of the whole. That's leadership.

Moving to the other belt-tightening message, here's how to wrap it up:

"Honey, I know we share a love of traveling, dining out, and occasionally splurging on a new piece of art. I also know we share a vision for what our retirement looks like, once the kids are grown, and that together we'll do what's needed to make that happen.

"The thing is, our CEO just told us that due to decreased sales revenues, we're going to have to cut corporate costs pretty significantly over the next six months. For now, he doesn't envision the need to let people go, so that's a good thing. That said, we're carrying some debt that would prove challenging if for some reason, I lose my job in the next year. The best thing for our future, I believe, is to be a bit more frugal with our spending and save as much as possible, just in case. That doesn't mean we're in trouble; it means we're being smart.

"I wish we weren't in this position and I understand this may feel unsettling – it does to me, too. I also have confidence in our ability to weather any storm together although this isn't one yet. I hope that being mindful about how we manage our money strengthens our family by giving us opportunities to be more creative and resourceful – this might be fun! I want to reassure you that we'll manage through together, like we always do.

"Here's what I propose. Let's put together a spreadsheet showing where we've spent our money over the last year or so, with no guilt involved. Then, let's individually look at what we can cut out for a while and make a plan for what we can give ourselves instead. As an example, for me, I could see giving up my Saturday morning golf outings and go for a morning bike ride instead – we could even do that as a family. I don't know what you might wish to cut, but I look forward to hearing your ideas, too. We might need to continue making modifications, but as long as we keep communication open, I know we can keep our finances in good shape. Who knows? Once we're out of this immediate situation, we may have saved up enough to go on that cruise we've always wanted to take."

Your spouse probably won't love this exercise, yet by saying what you're willing to do first, you're giving them personal choice too. And by articulating the possible long-term benefit of this financial restraint – a dream vacation – you're eclipsing short-term discomfort with long-term aspiration. Good job!

Talking to your child about a medical condition puts you in a position that might feel counter-intuitive – you're making yourself vulnerable and human when your instinct is to be the protector and provider. All of these can co-exist when communicated effectively:

"Sweetheart, I know you've been worried about how tired I've been lately, and I've seen you take on a lot more responsibilities around the house without being asked. I'm sure this has been bothering you more than you've said.

"Thank you for helping out. I'm proud of you. After telling Dr Jones how I was feeling, she ran some tests. I'm going to need surgery because I have a lump in my thyroid gland (*gesturing where the thyroid gland is*) that concerns her a bit. Right now, we don't know if it's something that may require further treatment, but we're getting it taken care of to be safe. So, next week, I'll be going to the hospital to have a minor procedure so we can find out what's going on.

"It's okay to be afraid, but I promise you that this family is strong enough to handle anything, right? I'm also excited that this will help me feel better, which will give me more energy to do all the things we love to do together.

"Here's what I can promise: no matter what happens next, I will tell you what's going on. I know I can count on you to tell me how you're feeling and to ask me anything you want to know, because that's the way this family rolls. But you know what I would like right now? To get a big hug from you!"

Children can sense when their parents are keeping secrets. Whether we realize it or not, we rob them of the opportunity to mature – to learn how to navigate through the unexpected challenges life offers – when we keep them in the dark about issues as important as the health of their parents. How much detail you provide will vary according to the age of your child(ren), but communicating what's happen-ing enables you to forge a closer bond that will serve you and your family well in the future. Finally, asking your child for a hug shows them that they can do something to help you, while simultaneously getting the reassurance they need.

"Hey, neighbor! I know you take incredible pride in your yard and garden – always so lovely! I also know that every Saturday, you like to get cracking early, before it gets too warm outside. Totally understand. This heat is crazy!

"I'm not sure you know, but I work until about 9pm every night during the week at the hospital, and I'm up early on Sunday to get to church, so Saturday is the only day I can sleep in. Between work and raising my kids, I need that extra rest to stay healthy and manage my responsibilities at home and at work. When you're tending your yard with the leaf-blower at 8am, it wakes up the household – children, husband, dogs and as a result, me – and I can't get back to sleep. I'd like to ask, quite respectfully, if you would consider either a later time or a different day to tend to your magnificent garden?

"I was worried about having this conversation because the last thing I want to do is offend or upset you; you all are such nice neighbors! And, I don't want to be one of those people, you know? I really appreciate your being open to changing your schedule a little bit, and for being so kind in this discussion.

"Would you be willing to use your leaf blower on another day or maybe later if Saturday is your preferred day? Also, if there's anything that we're doing that disturbs you, please do let us know because it's so important in this crazy world to have good neighborly relationships. Oh, and one last thing: what is your secret for getting your hydrangeas to bloom so beautifully?"

You might be tempted to add that you know he's retired and could do his yardwork during the week while you're at work, but that could serve to polarize him in his position. No one wins. Instead, you've invited him to hear your position and to respect your request with an agreement to revise his schedule. He may not know how much noise his leaf-blowing makes because he's wearing ear plugs. Through your approach, you've acknowledged what is important to him (a beautiful yard and garden), what is important to you (one morning to sleep in plus a good relationship with your neighbor), and offered him the opportunity to teach you about hydrangeas.

One final note: in each of these examples, I've concluded with either a call to action or a feedback loop. That is, "let's keep the lines of communication open." This step is vital in conveying to your audience that you're not trying to dictate the situation, but that you're presenting your perspectives and are giving them a safe place to present theirs too.

Amygdala Hijack averted.

10. Go with the Flow

In addition to helping your audience metabolize whatever difficult message you need to convey in a non-threatening manner that mitigates the Fight, Flight, Freeze or Fawn response, this communications methodology – once you've practiced a few times – begins to feel quite rhythmic and, dare I say, elegant. In summary, it's as simple as Know, Think, Feel, Do.

Begin with articulating what you know:

"I know there have been some questions/ concerns/ communication/ rumors about..."

Follow with how/what your audience needs to think:

"There are a few things you should know that help explain the context of this decision/ action, so here is the information that will give shape/context to this situation..."

Move toward what you imagine (and ultimately wish) your audience may feel:

"I understand this may be concerning (exciting, confusing), but I want to reassure you... I want you to be confident... I hope you share my excitement..."

Then, finish with what you want/need people to do and what you will:

"With all of this information, here are my expectations of what we need to do... as a next step... over the next six months... by this deadline... I will keep you posted... let me know if you have thoughts or questions."

As I shared earlier, I developed this methodology specifically for effective leader communications and quickly recognized its universal applicability to any emotionally charged situation. While teaching this methodology in a professional setting several years ago, I invited workshop attendees to challenge me – to present a real-life situation with which they needed to communicate the need for change – as a proof of concept. (There are always doubters.) In this particular session, I fielded several scenarios and used the "Know, Think, Feel, Do" approach quite effectively. Nods of affirmation all around. Good! Then a hand went up.

"So, here's one for you, Ms. Groves," the young woman said, standing up.

"My five-year old sneaks into the freezer when I'm not looking and eats as much of the ice cream as she can before someone catches her. My older kids get furious because there's not enough for them, and all hell breaks loose."

All eyes looked at me as if this might be the scenario that would break my methodology.

"Okay, that does sound like a challenging situation!" I answered with a smile. "Any particular flavor of ice cream?"

"Doesn't matter," Weary Mom replied, shaking her head.

"First, it's best to crouch down so you are eye to eye with your kiddo, yes? Okay, here goes. 'Honey, I've noticed that we seem to be going through a lot of ice cream and there's not always enough for the rest of the family after dinner. I know how much you love ice cream… I mean, who doesn't? (Know)

"But here's what I need you to understand. The rest of the family loves ice cream too, and they get really upset when we don't share things fairly. (Think)

"I know how much you love Blue Bell, and that you'd feel sad if your sisters ate all the Cookies and Cream and didn't leave any for you, right? (Feel)

"Here's what we're going to do, and I need your help. You get to be in charge of asking the family each week what flavor of ice cream you want me to get at the store, then you're going to help me scoop the ice cream into bowls for everyone after dinner so we all get our fair share. How does that sound?" (Do)

The woman nodded appreciatively, then said it hadn't occurred to her to give her five-year old the chance to contribute to the choices or a solution because as a mother, she had been more intent on discipline – the old command and control. It doesn't work with anyone, not if what you're seeking is engagement and strengthened relationships versus being in charge. The two concepts can co-exist, but only through effective communication based on constructive intent.

11. Physician, Heal Thyself!

You've now been given the formula to communicate difficult or challenging messages using *Know, Think, Feel, Do*, and your relationships with others will surely benefit. But what of your relationship with yourself? Do you employ a consistent form of self-talk when facing life's messiness?

I can say with certainty that I'm harder on myself than I am on others, perpetually susceptible to my own inner critic, judge and jailer. Does that sound familiar? I also allow my own amygdala to be hijacked more than I like to admit when I don't take the methodical steps to stop and evaluate the situation. A mentor of mine once advised me to "slow down to speed up," and it's a terrific philosophy, if followed.

When presented with a daunting professional change, an overwhelming personal obstacle, the results of a mistake you've made, or even an unexpected ghosting by a friend or lover, you may devolve into a litany of negative self-talk that steeps you in miserable self-loathing.

It doesn't have to be this way! The first step is to slow down. Slow *waaaay* down, and speak to yourself differently.

Carl Jung developed the concept of the 'inner child' as part of his divine child archetype, and his philosophy is still widely employed among psychotherapists today. Quite simply, if we were parented in such a way that we were ignored, criticized excessively, denied our genuine emotions, or left to sort out the complexities of maturing on our own, our inner child was forever left longing for gentle and compassionate parenting.

And even if your parents were nurturing and supportive as you navigated life's challenges, you may still forget that when you're frightened or anxious, your inner youngster needs to be soothed. In these moments, you can employ this same methodology – Know, Think, Feel, Do – in your self-care.

Doing so then allows you to calmly evaluate what you know or have observed, determine what additional information or context you might need, acknowledge how the situation is making you feel, and then identify how to proceed.

Let's start with your work environment. You've just learned that your boss is retiring, and while you're qualified to apply for his position, you also recognize the CEO typically hires senior executives from outside the organization rather than promoting from within. And who's to say your boss's replacement won't want to build their own team instead of working with the talent already in place? You've been with the organization for nearly ten years, but with news of your boss's departure, you fear you may have reached your maximum potential there. Your mind races as you try to peer into an imaginary crystal ball for clues about how all this will affect you. Meanwhile, your daughter is showing you brochures of expensive universities she's interested in attending next year.

Are you sweating yet?

Don't.

Stop, breathe, and put *Know, Think, Feel, Do* to work for yourself.

"Self," you might say, "Bob just told me he plans to retire at the end of the month. He decided it was time, particularly since he hasn't been in the best of health, to enjoy life for a change. (This is what you *know*.)

"I would be interested in applying for the position, yet we don't have a succession plan in place, so Stan may do what he always does and look outside the company for Bob's replacement. Bob hasn't been happy for the last year or two and it's taken a toll on him and the entire department. I wonder if it was his health or the politics that led him to announce his retirement? (Here are things to *think* about for additional context.)

"I feel conflicted. First, I'm sad Bob is leaving; he was a supportive boss who helped me grow in the organization. Beyond that, while my ego desires the bigger title and corresponding salary, do I really want the headaches associated with senior management? I'm also scared that a new vice president might not think I'm good enough and replace me with someone else younger and less expensive. With Jana heading to college next year, the thought of being unemployed worries the hell out of me. (You're acknowledging all the ways this situation makes you *feel*.)

"So for now, I'm going to focus on what I *can* control. First, I'm going to schedule an appointment with Bob to ask what additional skills I may need in order to be considered for his position, and any additional advice he might offer. Next, I'm going to commit time to writing a comprehensive list of my accomplishments since joining the company, and I'm going to compile a file of samples to illustrate the quality of my work. From there, I'm going to update my resume and begin perusing job boards, just to know what opportunities are out there. I might even apply for a few. Finally, I'm going to schedule a team building event so the folks in my division can discuss Bob's departure and any concerns they might have." (You've established a tangible list of what you can *do* to manage yourself through the imminent change.)

Here's another example. Imagine you just had to have your beloved pet euthanized after a lengthy and expensive series of cancer treatments. Your company does not grant bereavement leave for those who have lost pets, and you feel foolish taking sick time because you might really need it in the future. Plus, you don't know how to explain the depth of your loss and how it's affecting you, and people might judge what they see as your over-reaction. She was only a dog, right? So why can't I just suck it up?

Start with what you know. "Ever since I adopted Bella from the animal shelter, she has been my constant companion and my greatest comfort. I did everything I could to get her the treatment she needed, but I finally needed to make the humane decision to end her suffering." (You have acknowledged what you *know*: Bella was a blessing in your life, and you took the best possible care of her for as long as you could.")

"While there may be people who judge me for grieving her loss as though she were a person, the fact is, losing a pet can be even harder than losing a friend or family member because of the unconditional love they offer. Not to mention, the daily routines associated with caring for the beloved animal, including their excitement when we get home from work each day. It's a deafeningly silent absence." (Here, you've provided yourself an accurate way to *think* differently about others' possible judgment based on the truth of your experience and that of others who have also lived with the loss of a beloved animal.)

"I feel guilty that I couldn't have done anything more to save Bella, and I can't imagine ever loving an animal this way again. Just looking at her bed makes me cry, yet my feelings are real and normal and don't have to be justified to anyone else. I'm not going to rush the grieving process, no matter what others may think." (You've know given yourself permission, free of outside opinions, to own how you *feel* for as long as you *feel* it.)

"I think it's important that I honor how important Bella was to me, so I'm going to take a few sick days from work to give myself room to process this loss. Then, I'm going to take a batch of homemade cookies to my vet's office. They took wonderful care of Bella, all the way through our goodbye, and will appreciate their dedication being acknowledged. Next, I'm going to make a donation to the shelter where I adopted Bella, perhaps even to help a dog needing heartworm treatment, so that animal has the same chance Bella did to find a loving home. Finally, I'm giving myself permission to honor my feelings as they arise, without judgment or negative self-talk. And when I'm ready, no matter when, I'll also give myself permission to be rescued by another dog, knowing I can never replace Bella." (Now, you've determined positive things you can *do* not to expedite the grieving process, but to accept it while extending kindness to others. Just as Bella did.)

Another example. What if the person you've been seeing for the past two months suddenly stops responding to your calls and texts, even though you had been in daily contact since your first date? You haven't had much luck with romantic relationships since your divorce, and now this person with whom you seemed to have a lot in common has disappeared with no explanation. You wonder what's wrong with you and why love is so elusive.

In this example, it's important to stay grounded in your perspective since you can't know theirs.

"While I was reluctant to turn to dating websites to meet people, my career is demanding and I vowed never to become involved with a co-worker. I don't have much time for other activities that would allow me to interact with new people, so exploring online platforms seemed the best option. (You've established what you *know* about your situation, desires, and motives for putting yourself 'out there'.)

"The thing is, it's hard to really know a person's character based on a few pictures and a profile summary. While I really thought this person matched most of what I put on my 'ideal partner' list – they had everything I told myself I wanted – I don't have to accept this ghosting behavior as normal in today's dating scene. (Here, you've given yourself a broader context in which to *think* about the other person's behavior, which you've appropriately deemed unacceptable.)

"My feelings are hurt though, because I really liked them. I assumed we were seeing each other exclusively, so I stopped accepting other invitations, and now I feel foolish. I'm also angry they didn't think I was worth any type of explanation and just disappeared into thin air. Ever since my divorce, I've wondered if I'd ever find love again. While this wasn't love – at least, not yet – I really liked them. And although I really want to know why they vanished, I'm not going to grovel. I'm better than that. (You've now given voice to the myriad emotions you *feel* – sadness, embarrassment, anger, loneliness, and curiosity – while simultaneously reinforcing your self-esteem by setting boundaries.)

"For now, I think it's best that I focus my energies on activities I can enjoy alone or with friends. I haven't been to an art museum in ages, and I'd love to explore a new hobby like throwing pottery or learning watercolor painting. I think I'll go online and see what classes the local community college offers, then I'm going to schedule a lunch and museum date with my pals. I'm not going to put my life on hold while waiting for true love to come knocking! There's too much I want to do to let this situation define me."

(Congratulations! Instead of consuming countless cartons of Rocky Road ice cream while crying in bed, you have instead identified healthy, life-affirming things you can *do* to enrich your life. You are worth it)

The way we talk to ourselves is every bit as critical – if not more so – than how we communicate with others. Consider your intent – keeping yourself from spiraling with worry, guilt, anger, sadness, etc. – and you'll see that *Know, Think, Feel, Do* will do wonders for your mental state when facing difficult life situations.

What are some challenges you're currently navigating? Use the following pages to practice this methodology yourself.

Cheat Sheet

My objective in writing this guide is to help take the stress from potentially charged situations so you can stay focused on avoiding Amygdala Hijack. And instead, understand how you and your audience can tackle the situation you're managing in a productive, respectful, and healthy manner. With practice, it will come naturally.

Here's a summary action list for any situation:

1. First, write a short sentence or two about what you hope will result from the messages you need to share. Are you wanting to harness opportunities, overcome obstacles, change behaviors, or mitigate conflict? What does a positive outcome look like in this situation?

2. Then, make a bullet point list of everything you know about the issue(s) needing to be addressed, any rumors circulating about this

situation, and/or possible misconceptions and pain points affecting your audience.

3. Next, make a bullet list of the key messages you want your audience to think about so they can genuinely internalize and understand the situation.

4. Referring to the pain points affecting your audience, either by the situation or the decisions you have made to address it, list how you believe they might feel, as well as how you're feeling about the situation.

5. From there, list what you need your audience to do in specific terms, as well as what you can sincerely commit to doing to keep them apprised of progress, additional changes, and outcomes. Do not forget to provide a mechanism through which your audience can provide feedback, ask questions, or offer suggestions going forward.

6. Finally, schedule future check-in discussions or communiques to keep your audience engaged, whether the situation is resolved, needs further course correction, or is still ongoing. Remember to acknowledge your audience's efforts to work toward the solution. Everyone likes to be recognized.

Most people – particularly those in positions of authority – believe their communication skills are adequate, if not solid. But have you found yourself needing additional conversations to clarify what you meant by what you said, or to further explain why you've asked for certain changes in actions or behaviors? Have you witnessed your audience misconstrue what you've communicated and fail to proceed as you've requested? Consider for a moment how much more effective you can be as a leader, spouse, parent, friend, if you avoided the perils of miscommunication by following these four steps. Life would be less stressful.

Changing how you've always communicated might feel daunting, particularly in critical situations and particularly if you've never been coached to change up your style. It's hard to incorporate a new process. and remember that communication is more about what the audience can and will process, than reacting to your own emotions or needs.

However, if you follow these four steps, you'll find difficult conversations more navigable, while conveying that your audience's needs matter to you.

Know, Think, Feel, Do.

Bravo for embarking upon your new path.

Practice

Have you ever attended a professional conference, gained valuable new insights, promised you would incorporate them back at home, then didn't, because you had no immediate need? It happens to the best of us, which is why I recommend using these prompts to practice the four-step methodology so it becomes part of your brain's 'muscle memory' and is there when you need it. You could also work with your colleagues to brainstorm potential situations – no matter how ridiculous – and apply *Know, Think, Feel, Do* so it becomes part of your team's culture. Wherever you are and whenever you can, please practice.

Situation: The woman in the cubicle next to yours continues to have loud personal conversations on her cell phone, making it difficult for you to concentrate. You don't want to tattle to your supervisor or HR, and you find earphones uncomfortable. What is your intention? To be able to do your best work while preserving your relationship with her.

Situation: Your seven-year-old comes home from school crying that Jason just told him there's no such thing as Santa Claus, and that he's a baby if he still believes. Your intention? It might be finding a gentle way to explain that Santa Claus is a symbol for the magic and generosity parents wish to show their children at Christmas. It also might be helping your child understand that just because other people believe certain things, it doesn't mean it's necessarily right for everyone.

Situation: You arrive at the hospital because you've been notified that your elderly mother took a nasty fall and she's waiting to be admitted. She's clearly in pain but the ER staff aren't being attentive. You've now been there for more than two hours and she hasn't been seen by a doctor. What is your intention? To acknowledge the ER is short-staffed and there might be more critical cases requiring their attention, while advocating for her comfort and care.

Situation: Your supervisor continually acknowledges the quality of your work and promises to provide you additional resources, as well as a promotion, to reward your contributions. Yet, months pass with no action on his part. Your intention? To have these commitments honored, or to understand why there's been a delay, while respecting his authority (and maintaining his support).

Situation: You and your partner have agreed to invest in having your kitchen renovated. After you've selected your contractor and reviewed the estimate, you see that to include what you want – custom cabinets and a chef's-grade gas range – and what she wants – Travertine tile and a double-convection oven – exceeds your budget significantly. Your intention? To find a compromise that will work for both of you, ensuring neither person feels they've been overruled.

Situation: You have a higher-ranking colleague in another department with whom you must collaborate in team settings, yet she routinely overrides your professional expertise in favor of her personal opinions, making it difficult for you to gain the team's consensus and do the job for which you're paid. What is your intention? To recognize she wants to have her opinions considered while requesting a more collegial approach that includes respecting your position and its scope of responsibility; and you want an agreement about how you can collaborate more effectively for the good of the organization.

Situation: Your twenty-something son just lost his job with few prospects on the horizon, and he's already struggling under student loan debt with no money in savings. He's asked to move back home after eight years of you and your spouse enjoying your empty nest. You want to help him through his immediate struggles, but you don't want to be an indefinite crutch. Your intention? To offer support that honors the loss and uncertainty he's feeling, while establishing your and your spouse's expectations of how this short-term fix will serve everyone's needs.

Situation: Your widower father has begun seeing a much younger woman he met online and with whom he believes he's in love, yet you can plainly see that her only interest is his money. You're concerned she'll take advantage of him – possibly even coercing him to marry her – and you're sure she'll end up spending what he and your mom worked so hard to save. What is your intention? To recognize his loneliness and desire for companionship, while helping him safeguard his finances in a respectful manner that conveys your love, trust, and protection.

Your turn! Using the following worksheets, what are some potential scenarios you can imagine that would enable you to put *Know, Think, Feel, Do* to work?

Practice

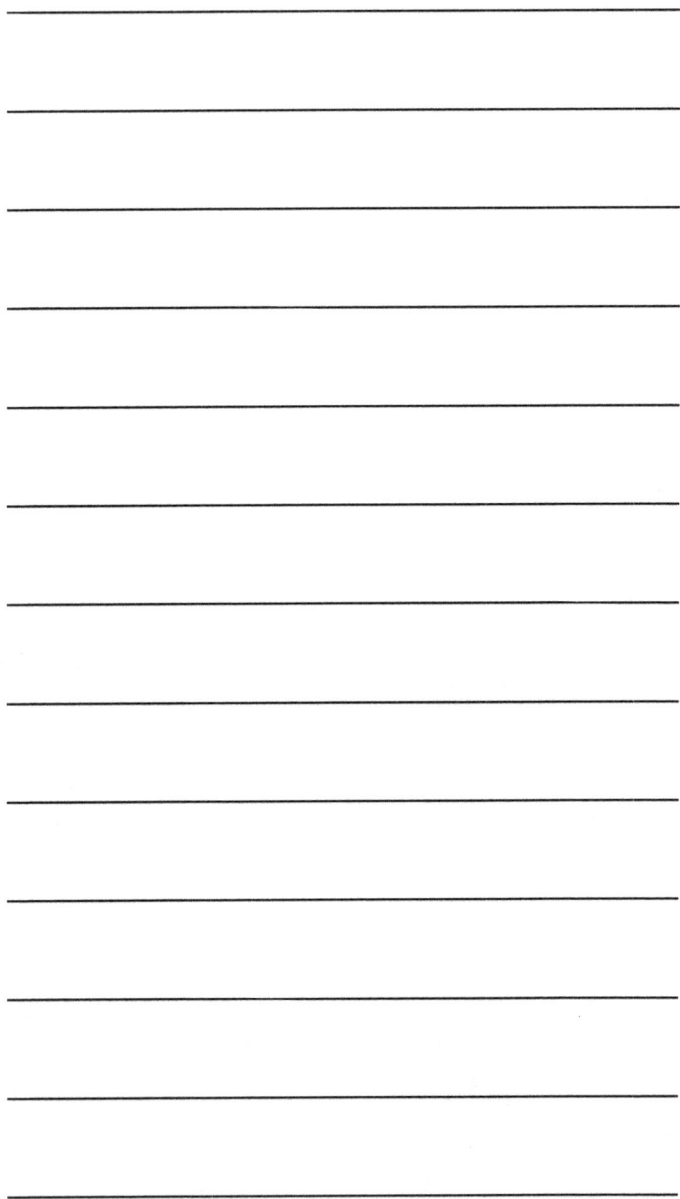

Acknowledgements

While I've contemplated putting this communications methodology on paper for years, I credit my husband, Noble Groves, for giving me the not-so-subtle push (and subsequent room) to put fingers to keyboard and get it done. Always my anchor, his support made all the difference.

My co-conspirator on all things writing related, Gin Coleman provided encouragement and periodic doses of "real talk" (delivered with love) when I needed it. Thanks, Gin!

All thanks to Reagan Rothe and his team at Black Rose Writing for helping me birth and raise this baby. The publishing world is fraught with unexpected dangers; thank you for being a safe place!

Finally, I'd like to give a big shout-out of appreciation to my best friend, Sheila Sinclair, for cheering me on as I finished each chapter and subsequently, the entire book. You'll get a free copy or two.

About the Author

Over the course of her 35-year career as a professional communications strategist, Suzanne Seifert Groves has managed and led every aspect of corporate communications, having served in leadership roles with several large organizations spanning multiple industries

In 2020, she was named a 'Top Woman in Communications' in the Visionary category by Ragan Communications/PR Daily in the inaugural year of the award.

Though passionate about the innate power of words used intentionally and effectively, Groves has yet to figure out how to use *Know, Think, Feel, Do* on her two German Shepherd dogs and recalcitrant cat, with whom she and her husband share their home in Arlington, Texas.

Contact her at: suzanne.s.groves@gmail.com.

Note from Suzanne Seifert Groves

Word-of-mouth is crucial for any author to succeed. If you enjoyed *We Need to Talk*, please leave a review online—anywhere you are able. Even if it's just a sentence or two. It would make all the difference and would be very much appreciated.

Thanks!
Suzanne Seifert Groves

We hope you enjoyed reading this title from:

BLACK ❧ ROSE
writing™

Subscribe to our mailing list – *The Rosevine* – and receive **FREE** books, daily deals, and stay current with news about upcoming releases and our hottest authors.
Scan the QR code below to sign up.

Already a subscriber? Please accept a sincere thank you for being a fan of Black Rose Writing authors.

View other Black Rose Writing titles at
www.blackrosewriting.com/books and use promo code
PRINT to receive a **20% discount** when purchasing.

www.ingramcontent.com/pod-product-compliance
Lightning Source LLC
Chambersburg PA
CBHW070549030426
42337CB00016B/2412